Big Feelings

Big Feelings

ISBN: 978-1-7324986-6-2

Cover design by Pablo Adriel Martinez.

Cover layout by Pablo Adriel Martinez, Josh Savory, and Kaleigh O'Keefe.

Edited by Liv Mammone, Story Boyle, Michael Malpiedi, Kelly Whelan and Josh Savory.

Formatted by Josh Savory.

Game Over Books
www.gameoverbooks.com

to the ones who give me the biggest feelings: noel quiñones, thank you for seeing me, black nail polish & all, these poems would not exist without you. gabe ramirez, you are my grandest teacher, i learned it all from you. to danyeli rodriguez del orbe, alejandro heredia, tammy lopez & sergio jimenez, thank you for reminding me how very much i have to learn. for keeping me accountable. for allowing me to shine. to devin devine, clementine von radics & sabrina benaim, you are worth 1000 spicy ketchups! to rebecca rivera, golden & lia hagen, you showed me my truest self in a basement with moscato & secrets. thank you for showing me what winning feels like. to glori b, and the austin poetry slam, thank you for being my safe haven when i really really needed one. to desiree dallagiacomo & my thoi cohort, thank you for helping to be strong right before all the really really hard choices i had to make. thank you for your blood moon light & love. to andrea gibson, it is truly unreal to know you. thank you for believing in me, and for your endless kindness. to lauren zuniga, forever hero, thank you for seeing all my glitter and being the og bloombox. to olivia gatwood, if i had to trace back where this all started, a big part of it is with you. thank you for continuing to inspire, staying strong, and showing us how wide our dreams can reach. to lydia andrews, my dear friend, the world is lucky to hold your voice, all of your endless soft. to rachel mckibbens, thank you for paving the way for all the cholas with big unapologetic hearts. blud stays on my altar for the moments i have to remember how to conjure fearlessness. to my pink door coven, thank you for showing me how to truly get free. to jay ward, liv mammone, madeline lessing, adrienne novy, cocoa flo, akeem rollins, stephanie westgate, anita dias, kay mcclendon, chance bell, benedicto figueroa, ilyus evander, leonard madrid, moria perr-e, daniel garcia, jon barr, mary ayala, and everyone who has believed that i could do the thing, i really really could not do it without you. to pablo, you make beautiful things. thank you for bringing my weird brain to life. to josh savory (editor extraordinaire + pending cookie accomplice) & the entire game over books team, thank you thank you thank you for seeing me. to my parents, my brothers, my sister, my mima, my granny, my family, i would not be without you. to marty, my love, we so deserve each other. to ducky, this book is about how i learned unconditional love from u lil squancheroon. to de la rosa mazapan, fenty highlight, the j train, the horchata truck off the kosciuzko stop, giant sweatshirts, new york city, milk bar, and all the other shit that got me through, i love u. listen, i never planned to release a book literally in the middle of a fucking pandemic. my world has ended over & over & over again. i was in abusive situations while i wrote this book. i was homeless when i submitted it. the world is always ending but somehow it's weirdly never all the way over. we only have each other & our stories & our reckless dreams. we are all just a big tangled ball of our big big feelings. trying to move forward. whether that means mapping a route to the moon or watching frozen II beneath a mermaid blanket. begin wherever you are. may the stars & lip gloss kisses & your favorite cereal rise to greet you. i am so glad you are here. thank u.

a crown of sonnets
for the empress of break-ups

stranger things suite

i say i have never climbed a tree before
& i haven't / never was a monkey bar jungle gym fortress of upper
body strength/not the pretty friend just the gateway / friend helping
boys put zots in kasey clingman's / mouth during drama class
holly fedor's 7th grade wingman / our entire class lined up / to sadie
hawkins her while she stayed late / to girl giggle at mr. lytle / it was
a wednesday / in 7th period & we were watching osmosis jones &
garrett was walking toward my desk but / garrett never talked to me
before like why / would garrett come to my desk? / & anyway he
asked me if i wanted to go out with his best friend / liam / i said yes
because he was tall & we laughed in biology once / over dead cats / &
i liked that & liam kissed me / by the portables once & i never forgot it
because every kiss before it was bad & i was like / 14 & we held hands
/ on the way to gym class he told me / his brother was sick like /
the sad kind of sick / his mom was sleepless & wailing / he came back
from the weekend / on crutches / broken leg / straight line for a mouth
& the bruja in me felt like all my bad / ugly haunted was making bad
things happen / to him / original ghost / i stopped talking to him / at
passing period / walked further ahead (he was on crutches so / i knew
he couldn't [catch me]) / tried to ignore / the christmas present he left / in
my locker / a small leather purse filled / with what i can only assume / was
the rest of his allowance / when the cast finally came off he caught up
/ i just told him that i didn't want to be his girlfriend & that wasn't
the truth i just thought / he would think i was / stupid for trying to
save him from / every stupid bad thing & / i have never climbed a tree
/ the only way to get back down is to fall / break / a bone & i feel like
nobody saves the sidekick / queen of / not cool / too soft / for her own
good / i feel like falling is all i know like trying / to save everyone is a
serious mission / i was never assigned like / if i never climb maybe /
    i'll save myself / instead

luz/gus

burque love is aaaalllll fucked up it's like buggin' someone
                until they get all butthurt or like peepee hearted or something
        it's like telling them to get down from the car at the dog house
    on ur first date & u stand next to em & ur short & they're like all tall
    but u figure it out anyways u go to sonics for a shake & hold hands
        or whatever but it's not like ur in love or nothing but ur friends
                                        are all like eeeeeeeeeeeee
that fool is cute &
        u know it in ur heart that the fool is actually real cute the first time u
    met was at drama fest in that weird little cow town at eastern when u
                        were like in high school or something
    & u were playing all these weird theater kid games where u had to like
                moo at each other & stuff & that fool
                    had the best moo like for real
        if they were a cow they would jump all high over the moon
    because they're a fuckin overachiever like that but anyways now
    it's been like a long time and ur all serio & stuff and the future is a big
    deal it's fuckin' scary man but u known this fool for so long & they're
                the only person who makes u feel like
                                    the sandia mountains or like
    ur mom singing mariachi in the kitchen or like three drinks at anodyne
        they're the only fool who makes u feel like that like ur a ghost but a
                        really cool fancy one
who's dead in the best way like u can be everyone
            who came before u but also urself that fool makes u feel
                    like good palo santo or like
        there's a luminaria in ur heart and it ain't even christmas that fool
                    makes u feel like a #9
easy green breakfast burrito from golden pride when ur like the most
                                            homesick
    like chile from hatch
    like ur mom's posole like a new mexican watercolor sunset
                        yeah like all that shit
                            but ur not in love or nothing

honest sonnet

i don't separate my laundry colors
i only floss when the dentist makes me
i got cheated on at prom but that was
not even the worst part. i cry a lot.
i miss the way my engagement ring felt
i sit on the bathroom floor when i'm sad
i only like the brooklyn bridge when i
go there alone. that's how i like most things
i don't miss being engaged to that man
i have said *i love you* on the third date
fucked on the first.
written songs right after.
i'm sure i've already felt everything
that's a lie. i was sure until today.
no one's ever looked at me like you do.

brown boy. the first time i saw you i thought you were short. i remember seeing you walk through two giant glass doors. your magic mike arms busting out of your tank top. two stars tattooed on either shoulder. a third one twinkling in your smile. i always dreamed i'd discover my own constellation one day. never knew one person could become the entire sky. how all the fuckboys are eclipsed by a breakfast in the morning kind of love. by kisses on the forehead & midnight true crime marathons or the way you hold me in your sleep like letting go is not an option. like so much has been taken from you already. brown boy. dreamer. when was the last time you slept peacefully enough to dream? i remember the morning you came home a ghost. where a ticket for a minor offense & a courtroom became the set of your very own american horror story & DACA was the middle name you didn't want me to know about. on September 5th, 2017, Deferred Action for Childhood Arrivals was repealed & the dream became a nightmare & the chase became a hunt. from now on i would only wake up to the sound of the modern day migra knocking at the door. wondering how i would cry if they took you away. if my cries would sound the same as your sister's or your mother's. i do not believe in marriage. do not believe in giving my heart to a government that only wants to cut it in half & call me commodity. but today, i am merely a woman who loves you more than all of the rainbows. merely a universe that could not exist if its entire sky disappeared. call me protector. call me warrior. call me your wife. i vow to be the answer to every last one of their uncomfortable questions. i vow to shove this nation's matrimony law back up its racist ass. you didn't want us here? well, that's too bad 'cuz we're here to stay. & tr*mp ain't invited to our brown-as-fuck fiesta of the century. when he said taco trucks on every corner, he was talkin about our wedding day. all the bachata & two step. the way we hold each other too close when we dance like only we know how our people paint death on their faces to prove they are unafraid to look it in the eye. they cry gritos to the wind for the familia lost to the border, to ICE, to the monsters with guns & privilege & serious white faces but tonight, we celebrate because they have never gotten rid of us before & sabes que they sure as hell won't start now. i vow to hold you close through the heavy knocks at the door. i vow to keep singing. i vow to keep fighting. for better or for worse. in sickness & in health. te amare.

three in the morning

i feel small when her name pops up on the screen seven years to my one it says she facetimed him says she's been thinking about him a lot lately i am a spiral of instagram and mutual facebook friends i am the crazy girl everyone says i am counting the number of little red hearts he saved up to give to her instead cardi b says it's ok to go through his phone so i do we used to walk the dogs together he walks the dogs alone anxiety bitch i become a tremor when i see how many times he's called her my depression is a stalled three train never knowing when i will go forward again everyone congratulates you it is all you can do to not get buried in all of their expectations in the outfits the wins the kisses on the cheek my depression does not know what is real and what isn't it believes that you don't really love me that no one does how could they? when you ask me what i'm going through i don't know how to be the pretender small shriveled clean lipstick smile kiss goodnight i am scouring my contacts for someone i can call at three in the morning the suicide hotline is always there i feel like a burden even to them imposter syndrome tells me that everyone will see what i am soon there is no good garden here i have imagined myself a kind of sick that unglues the fake lashes wipes away the glitter unsnatches something already stolen i want to legally change my name to g.g.—ghost girl—when they ask what my initials stand for i will tell them nothing i will tell them something used to be there but i can't find it anymore do you know how many people have told me that they don't want me when i am sad? i tell them this is the only way that i know how to be they retweet about celebrities lost to this disease they post the crisis hotline not their own number they close all the spaces they held for me once i am just a phone that rings with no answer i evaporate into the ghost that they have made me into nothing or smoke wake up the next morning dunkin donuts iced coffee myself into novacaine force my wired shut jaw to chew eat breathe i will breathe like a burning house uncertain it will ever be anything other than flame billowing i fell for twelve hours yesterday no one to catch me cried until my body renamed itself pillar of salt after looking back too many times ignoring the fires tattoo the words "it's not my fault" on every square inch of me i still do not believe it

I. on the drive back,

i see stars for the first time in months
i think about the cloud echoes of city
garbage streets
permeating the summer
stars in new york city
can only be seen
attached to commercials
youtube red ads in times square
i think about the mister softee truck
from last summer
how it came out of hibernation
just before i left
the driver remembered me
our exchange of spiderman paleta
brown joy
ninety degree sticky sweat
clung to our inflatable
swimming pool bodies

II. i cannot stop itching
my mother asks me
not to be at a protest
picket at the border checkpoint
asks me not to say
any of that american studies stuff
it is a joke and we laugh
until my body becomes amoeba riot
writhing
under a fluorescent microscope
they examine a long line of cars
one after the other
waving them through
a flicked wrist and a puckered lip
apologizing for any inconvenience
i see the agent's hands
change their tone
start speaking in caps
they speak in code
to the men in the booth
the uniformed man says
roll down the window
stay still, answer my question
listen to my voice
says stop
just stop

III. my mother tells me about
the last time
they stopped my brother
he will drive through again
next week
last time
they assumed his spanish
bear trapped his running tongue
wouldn't stop asking him
where home was

IV. i tell my boyfriend about the stars
how easy they are to see
in a blank canvas desert
i think about him
bundled on the couch in brooklyn
how safe he is
i see a falling star for the first time
wish that those patrol hands
anxious to take
never look at him too long
i wish there were no hungry hands
to worry about
no fluorescent lights
only stars

ode to ducky
the bodega kitten

to paws dipped in milk
      like forever socks
      like miniature whiskers
freckled mouth with baby dinosaur teeth
i only got out of bed today
to watch him snatch a ribbon
to google whether or not it was ok to feed him pepperoni

      i have not slept
      nights full of manyness
      &missing the boy
      &loneliness
      &unbeing
      i children's benadryl'd my wine
      did the sad drinking thing
      they tell you not to do
      i have never been maternal
      not even to myself

tonight
he paws and kneads his way
onto my bosom
      nah, fuck that
my titty shelf
tucks his soft monster head into decolletage
&kitties himself into dreaming
his toy drum heart
beating
telling me stories
of how he survived this big trash city
whispering
look at how we made it here together
reminding me that
feeling small
only means that i am
so so alive

14

a lyric ghazal of ariana grande albums for the boys we lose

i have spent so many days
waiting for you to break free
the nights i would pray that
your broken wouldn't break me

thought i would be yours, truly
i couldn't stop your breaking
why did you ever choose her?
dangerous woman breaks you

how is the high prettier
than me asking you to stay?
what did you need me to be?
restless heart you can't make free

no tears left to cry, i thought
new love; departure from grief
boy, you were my everything
unexpectedly set free

and now, god is a woman
i wish you had listened to
wishing death wasn't the way
broken boys chose to get free

a crown of sonnets for the empress of break-ups

a sonnet for the rebound

white boy says *i'm sorry* says if i need
to get a hold of him i can message
him on linkedin / white boy leaves nice voicemails
calls me at seven on his way to work
white boy is lucky i had to be up
anyway / he calls me out of worry
i remember worrying about him
white boy said nothing / watched my therapist
pick his name out of wet tissue and blood
i am dancing on a grave / is this love?
or assimilation / a cracked empire
luxuriating a lover who will
not understand me / one who will erase
my name by simply saying it out loud

for the good date

i love the way you say my name out loud
this bar brings out all your travieso
hanes white t-shirt, hair, slicked back. mango tree
tattooed next to an obvious love song
they warned me about your smile. heartbeat. laugh.
still want you to bathroom graffiti me
sharpie what you can't tell anyone else
whispering a recipe for heaven
to the back of my jaw 'til i echo
maybe we are both just disappointing
sad. surrounded by putting green regret
tonight, my sickness renamed itself hope
the only disappointment is with those
who wallow in letting us go too fast

for all the things i can do now

it happened fast. shaved the side of my head.

it felt the same as piercing my septum.

or the time i wore a mesh see-through shirt.

cropped.   open and soft.   all bra obvious.

i memorize everything you don't like.

now, i do it all because you are gone.

you take leave and i have a new closet.

a new nose full of sterile stainless steel.

i will get another bruja tattoo.

cry all the ways you didn't want me to.

remove the words *calm down* from new men's mouths.

rewind the pillow thrown into the lamp.

    the nights you unmissed me 'til 4 a.m.

      stop saying, *I don't really know what to say*

half-sonnet for what broke

i dont really know what to say except
that i love u & i want to keep fight
ing for this & putting things back toge
ther i saw the beer in the fridge i thought
u said u had stopped pleasedontstartagain
i dont love u anymore but i dont
want u to drown urself to death over—

FROM MY EX

I WANT YOU TO DROWN YOURSELF TO DEATH
I PUT YOUR BOOKS IN THE CORNER SO THEY
CAN THINK ABOUT WHAT THEY'VE DONE   LIAR WHORE
HEART FULL OF HORNETS   LEFT THE BED TAINTED
I KNOW YOU ONLY SEE ME AS A HOME
AND THAT WILL NEVER BE ENOUGH YOU KNOW
I WANT TO BE THE LOCK ON EVERY DOOR
THE LAST DROP OF WHISKEY ON EVERY MAN
YOU WILL EVER LOVE   I NEVER HIT YOU
ONLY CALLED YOU   WASTED   TO TELL YOU I'M
A GOOD MAN   TOLD YOU TO GROW UP
OUT LOUD UNTIL THEY CALLED SECURITY
WATCHED YOU CRY HARD WITH YOUR FAKE SPANISH TONGUE
I JUST WANT YOU TO LEARN WHAT YOU DESERVE

a phone call to my mom

i think i've fin'lly learned what i deserve
i promise i'm safe. i did have to leave.
things shoved into a corner. defaced love.
....
my roommate is cute. we might already
fall in a circle ... is this what i do?
occupy hearts with open vacancies?
....
the last man i loved offered empty rooms
i, stupidly, decorated; painted
the walls ... got comfortable ... called it home
the girl before hadn't even moved out
he told me that this was not a big deal
made me gargle mixed drinks ... vodka ... whiskey
alcoholism ruins a party
....
fuck the things in life we don't understand

for matches

my mom says the best things in life are   things
we don't understand. you   keep me so vexed
we talk for hours about ugly babies
acoustic showtunes, varied   broken hearts
every move,   breakfast cereal glucose
we moved in together on   our first date
your arms hold permanent stories;   hold me
shattered rose plant potted back together
never knew what roots could be, now I bloom
pray   at an altar of new white candles
light constellations ablaze.   yesterday,
when you looked at me,
        you made me a match
i hope that you never say *i'm sorry*

ariana + pete

ariana grande breaks up with pete davidson and louie says it's because of borderline personality disorder, says things never work out for guys like him and pete, says *that's what we do, we tattoo, we buy engagement rings, like the end is nowhere in sight,* the articles say she gave the ring back, she will keep the pet pig, the name tattooed on her ring finger, covered by a band-aid. A week after I met louie, I tattooed a heart on my knuckle to match one he already had, the skin has stretched, there are some wrinkles with no ink, I just want to remember that my joy is an imperfect permanence, to live in the recklessness of a love that falls so hard, it strikes the needle into portraiture. When I moved in, he said I could share his bookshelf, I noticed a spine etched with the words, *Loving Someone With Borderline Personality Disorder.* He has never stumbled into a bookstore and impulse bought, he is measured and meticulous, a curated single shelf. I know he bought this book on purpose. I want to know why it is so many chapters long, loving him is a book written overnight, an album of songs recorded on an iPhone, given as a gift, every track is named after him, I could say his name on every talk show, Instagram for all the stans who only want a knuckle tattoo love, one they can believe in, despite everything else, loving him is the easiest poem I have ever written, maybe we cry too much, we are over exposed nerve, soft, despite everything that has ever rendered us open wound, the angry sad pushes us to places we wish we didn't recognize, but damn, don't we deserve a love story too? Maybe, ariana and pete didn't make it, but we have to, there are so many matching tattoos to get, so much future to hold in our hands and marvel at, like we are so very rich in tomorrows, I will not stop bumping that Ariana album, the same way I ride for all of our reckless, this love could not be impermanent if it tried, I will sing its song, hope for all the good news articles to find us, I will keep the pig and the ring and all of the tomorrows I can fit in my pockets, I will love him hard and fast, reminding him every day, he makes all of it so so easy.

LOUIE SAYS WEIRD THINGS LIKE *will you go to the haunted penitentiary in philadelphia with me?* and *jimmy fallon is a talentless hack!* louie says things like tecate in a can and survivor is the best show on tv and let's build a shelter for dogs at the end of their lives and let them have a kick ass goodbye. let's call it our home. louie has a tattoo of virtue the cat telling its owner, *i know you're strong* louie says he has too many feelings. they are all too big to fit inside his thin mural body bursting with orchids for bones. he says a doctor told him so. so it must be true.

louie says weird things like: *i love you*
                             you're safe
                             i want to make you happy

i don't know how to tell him that everything sounds weird to me unless it is a broken chaos. police out a window. keys jingling on a boy chasing me from a bus stop. louie says weird things like *tomorrow* and *yesterday* and *so much time* and i wish i could give him all the days before this one and everything after. i don't know how to tell him that i have never wanted to sing along with the sound of someone's heartbeat so badly. that i am a writer who could not spell love until now. he's making me say weird things too like *i love you. we are going to make it.* makes me play all my old love songs like no one has ever broken my heart. i don't know who or what to believe. but i only want to believe all the weird wonderful. the everything that makes no sense. i will give myself to it. like broken was never a word to begin with. like i will only ever listen to all the weird things louie says and i will promise to only ever say weird things back.

i just hate it when people mispronounce my name like— it's really not that hard mmkay my name is **#BRENDA™**. upper west side Brenda™, nob hill Brenda™, clarksville Brenda™— hiiiiiii my name is Brenda™!!! i only live in neighborhoods where i can get a scalp massage immediately after hot yoga. my fiat needs an oil change so my husband, Brad™, said i should just get a new one. then i'll have like... three! i'm an amazon prime member so i get my $4 blueberries from whole foods for my daily! kale! smoothieee! call me keto diet Brenda™, lululemon Brenda™, shitting all my water weight Brenda™. i hate all those accessible bikes and scooters because like anyone can use them it just makes the neighborhood so urban. i only like "cardi b" when she sings about like feminism and like being a woman-y'know when it's like-comfortable for me but i mean i sing "i like it" at the wine bar with my #g-u-r-l-z, okuRRRR, ugh i can't do it! it's just so hard to roll my r's or like lift a finger or like see a world beyond the tiffany tennis bracelet on my wrist. the mexican coffee shop down the street used to be so dirty but like it's a starbucks now so who cares? i always get a venti gentrification or a grande neighborhood restoration with soy almond republican tendencies and light passive aggressive white supremacy— keeps me from getting bloated. i also liiiiive for rosé like YAAAASSS rosé! all! day! sometimes my drink of choice is a vodka soda, my drink of choice is white feminism, my drink of choice is affirming myself as the standard so that every other girl on the planet knows that she's just a supporting character in the world of Brenda™. every guy who's ever seen me wants to be with me and like how can i blame them? i am like painstakingly manic pixie perfect. meeting a non-brenda would mean having to understand a world outside of societal expectation. plus, i'm like so cute! have you seen my $90 haircut, my $90 manicure, my $90 lack of a soul. just want you to real housewife me, marry me until we separate until we are like nuclear family, until we are the measure of heteronormative caucasian perfection. i never asked to be special or different or like interesting. i just want everyone to stop calling everythingggg i do cultural appropriation. like everyone knows i created the world. it all belongs to me anyway. like would you go into a church & like start attacking god? all i ever did was teach the world how to be perfect and vote for hillary clinton and sing "fight song" in my car. all i ever did was name my baby Brindlington™ and stan scarlett johanssen and bulldoze everything that was here before to create a Kardashian paradise so yeah—i'm basically god and i'm just trying to order my effing starbucks on my way home from cycling class. all i ever did was ask you to get my effing name right.

WHITE BOY, UNINTERRUPTED

White Boy says,
I had to wait in line at Starbucks today, so I know about oppression
White Boy retweets NPR and watches Jeopardy for fun,
White Boy won't admit it but he likes when you get the answer wrong,
likes the feeling of knowing just a little bit more than you do
White Boy listens to indie music and paints his life
a *500 Days of Summer* shade of mope
because the whole world loves him the least
White Boy is glad *Parasite* won the Oscar
and not glad Tr*mp is the president,
not glad, but safe,
happy to know he will not have to live in a world
where white people are the minority,
White Boy says, *aren't you white?*
White Boy says he knows all about brown people
because of all the Spanish girls he's dated,
says real tacos have radishes on them,
says horchata is mexican titty milk
& i'm like, *damn, I wish my titties were full of horchata*
or maybe I don't because White Boy would just set me up
at a hipster cold brew coffee shop somewhere
& start turning a profit while I bust my horchi-chis
in another episode of cultural appropriation at its finest
White Boy thinks my brown mouth is dirty
with every flip of my chingona tongue
and every *fuck you!* shouted at the orange tv pendejo
White Boy thinks my brown mouth/my brown friends/my brown life
is dirty when I tell him that I am tied to this land, to my native Aztlan
blood and the red dirt in my teeth
White Boy responds by texting me a picture of a cartoon Pocahontas,
naked ass out, standing next to John Smith
who is holding a looped belt, smiling,
White Boy says *jk lol*,
White Boy thinks it'd be kinky
if I said *colonize me, daddy* right before he cums,
White Boy tells me this in a tinder message,
tells me he does not believe in privilege,
meaning it is not a privilege to love me

not a privilege to hold me or fuck me or whisper in my ear,
White Boy just expects these things, just like his ancestors did,
White Boy says he could beat me at a job interview
or a sport or a poetry slam
White Boy says he could beat me
White Boy says, *I don't need your consent, I'm your boyfriend*,
doesn't understand the word '*no*'
since he is the only one who ever gets to say it
White Boy tastes like expensive toothpaste and entitlement,
his favorite movies are *The Social Network* & *American Psycho*,
he jokes about luring me in like prey, tells me about the way bunny
rabbits are calmed to stillness and forced to trust,
just before someone slides the skin off their small bodies,
he tells me this while playing with my hair,
as I am splayed across his chest wondering why
I keep making the same mistakes over and over again,
he is so comfortable with the way history keeps repeating itself
& I just wanna kick and push my way out of his palms,
I am all bunny rabbit heartbeat and sudden will to live,
White Boy always leaves me hoping I won't have to run away
screaming this time, leaves me wishing he was better
than all of the men and mistakes before him,
White Boy says he is already the best there ever was

twitter sestina
for suicidal ideation

after ariana grande

when my brother said he didn't want to be anywhere
the concerned friend told the counselor, told everyone
a flurry of bored small-town cops knew they'd find him here
rename him psych ER, borderline, the places he'd be going
mansplain his illness to my mother, like she doesn't know anything
cry, synonymous with crime, not heard by anyone

i was never afraid of anyone
until my brother tore into traffic asking to be anywhere
my mouth, an archery of curse words & panicked anything
hollered across a winter gravel lot surrounded by everyone
we sauntered off, neither caring where the other was going
a restless surrender that i could never be here

not the way he needed me to be, louie never asks me to be here
i always am, i have never met anyone
who showed me all the everywhere i could be going
he is all the everything at once, a portrait of the anywhere
i stained glass all his broken into everyone
and only see him, i hope he knows i would do anything

so he'd wake up tomorrow, the men i love most would do anything
to run fast from the world, somewhere far from here
i know i can't be everyone
who made them feel like they weren't anyone
just want to take them away, anywhere
to light candles until they ask me where we are going

pete davidson instagrams about where he is going
he says *just know i told you so,* i want to hear anything
else, ariana tweets, he says he will not be anywhere
she is, sometimes, my heart is one elevator away, keeping me here
at the bottom, telling me he never needed me/anyone
i will still wait in the lobby despite everyone

and him, still try to be everyone,
to know where we are going
some days, i wish i could be anyone
just to give him anything
i am not already giving, sometimes love is to just be here
just staying when you could be anywhere

i'm downstairs and i'm not going anywhere
if you need anyone or anything
i know u have everyone u need and that's not me but i'm here too*

*the envoy is a tweet posted by ariana grande when she attempted to
see pete davidson due to his concerning Instagram post that implied
suicidal ideation

my boyfriend's ex-girlfriend has a tv show on bravo

and she is a self-proclaimed liberal/ socialist/ bartender/ lolita/ waving
a pride flag/ a convenient tombstone for her to weep at/ an identity
to wear long enough/ to host a queer open mic/ calls her ex's new
girlfriend/ whore/ slut/ still checks the box labeled/ fuck-you-feminist/
called me a/ scared kitten / once/ unwitting twenty something/ afraid of
her own skin/ i want to ask about her skin/ like how did she get it?/ her
costume/ the backstage of her/ white woman/ crusading to save middle
america/ or believe something good about herself/ that she is good/
says/ homo/ like you cannot spell it without the word/ home/ treats
the world like her personal/ cab driver/ just want to ask her if she has
ever known/ what it is to be a/ snake/ legless desert thing/ fighting for
your next meal/ child of a wasteland/ to live where your split tongue
is only/ evil/ learning to inhabit poison/ spit/ a name pressed out of
adobe/ written on/ a government form/ an incantation of blood/ a sound
they will rename silence/ erasure is/ not a brooklyn barrio/ asking for
a hand in gentrification/ trendy broken thing/ to put your name on
the waitlist for/ disadvantage plays hard to get/ oppression /that was
never there to begin with/ just want to explain all that/ ghost/ bartender
paychecks/ wasted on liquor/ dumped into a cab/ "thank you"/ tattooed
inside her bottom lip/ never leaving her mouth/ faker to all/ friend to
none/ some days/ my last name is a balance beam i keep falling off of/
afraid i will never know its story/ but at least i know my walk is never
performative/ i can see the end of my stride/ yolanda/ esperanza/ i will
find her someday/ bravo would never be interested in/ filming that
moment/ no one wants to fall in love with/ all this blood/ too messy/ let
them twitter hate the fake/ instead/ stay lost/ entertained by ghosts/ in a
lineage of nothing/ porcelain vanity circus/ funhouse mirror for a heart/
my boyfriend's ex girlfriend has a tv show on bravo/ pendeja/ i will still
watch the whole thing/ just to remember what it felt like/ to be hollow/
pretending/ before i cared/ about the way my name left/ the world's
mouth/ then learned to care more about/ the way it left my own

stranger things suite

"make mistakes, learn from them, and when life hurts you
(because it will), remember the hurt. the hurt is good. it means
you're out of the cave."
—jim hopper, stranger things

"we have shared trauma. what's a little more?"
—nancy wheeler, stranger things

max & i talk to our brothers, trapped in a sauna

hey. i hope you know i only did this because i love you.
we all just want this thing out of you &
i know there's part of you that does too.
that part isn't around much anymore & it's really hard &
anyway...i don't know. i know
you are my best friend. i know
there is only one brother like you.
i get so scared when i think of you
exploding.
boiling all because you were trying to shine too bright.
i have hated you.
friends don't lie.
i don't want to lie to you through this little window.
i know you know.
i can never hide from you. you, volume dial. all the way up.
loud belly scream.
i believe you. that you want to go. burst into a quiet nothing.
you don't do sadness.
i believe you. i know what it is to always live with your hand
on the doorknob. ready
to push. go. right now though, i hear you crying.
saying please & i am
begging you to close the gate. fight it with everything you are.
i can't sing a song over your casket. left behind.
knowing i never said everything
i was supposed to. please. i just
i just want my brother back

i was really upset about that/ wedding/
ex-boyfriend/ ex-best friend/
joined in holy cheatrimony/
& everyone was sure/ it was because of/
him/ even me/ she used to fly
around/ the world of a boy/ in two &
a half minutes/ twirl girl/ tuesday night
swing dance/ she gave me/ death cab/ poems/
good movie musicals/ taught me cool/ bad/
la vie boheme/ drama class/ flirt/ bird girl/
beautiful/ now/ they dance to/ our song/
band of horses/ two people i/ lovedlost &
just like always/ i keep waiting/ for her/ to
look at me/ instead/

tammy thompson

[good screams//bad screams]

i tell him, when you vote or
post on facebook about women's rights or
think about your mom & your sister
i want you to remember my face
right now, drenched in all my never
going back, they say la llorona drowned
her children over a man
wailing in the night, bad screams &
that's how i feel
like i am wringing water out of my poems when i try
to tell the nightmare of him, when i see his name
anywhere, the letters run together wet weeping
[the howl i hear in] thewordhome icouldn't [sleep]
forsolong [is it still a nightmare] i fit actuallyhappened?
[or just my] verylogicalbrain [praying to a] veryimaginary [god]
[to undo] acautionarypast? itried totellthem, spellitout
inchristmaslights, theyflooded [my sorry lips]
withtheir ownalphabet,
[said] nonothim childhoodfriend VeryTalentedPoet™
[he stole] foodfrommyfridge [once], lethimselfin [my home],
[was in jail] afewtimes [but]
[no], areyousureyouaren'tconfused?[mixing up bad screams]
&goodscreams? [what are good screams?] don'tyouknow?
[the ones you] askedfor? soobviously [wanted?][the only ones]
wewillaccept? closethegateonyou stayhaunted [no one can hear
you down there] anyway&if
[they're not listening] iguess
[they won't believe you]

justicia para barb

in old pictures, my mom kind of looks like barb from stranger things,
coke bottle lenses & a tablecloth floral in jewel tones all trapper keeper
& homework & curfew, calling home from a seven eleven payphone
after losing her keys at a prescription pill party she wasn't supposed to
be at, lying about a cash register so miraculously placed at amy's house
during their cheap fake lie of a slumber party, mint prom dress, lace &
long hepburn gloves, matching rubber band braces, i do not like to go
most places   alone
& neither does my mom & i guess
that's how we end up with each other but also   how we end up
                         with people we don't really want to be with
in places we don't really want to be & charlie was
on the football team & he was popular, popular charlie
with all his popular charlie friends
at the popular drill team formal my mom needed a date to &
she didn't really want to be there with popular charlie but   she still
was & that's, as the kids say, a mood & popular charlie thought
it was popular to ask for a kiss at the door & my unpopular mom
                                                            said no
which was very unpopular & popular charlie did the popular thing
                                 & did what he wanted
anyway, unleashed a small monster
in my mother's maw & anyway   assault is

like a swimming pool we get sucked into at
                         a party we didn't want to be at

& everyone says they can't find us but maybe
they just don't want to until   the monster's
too big inside us,   eating us alive
until he wins &   it's too late
& in these stories, i picture my mom kind of like barb
from stranger things & i guess i kind of look like my mom
& neither of us were very popular in high school

a note on justicia para barb:

my mom ran into not-so-popular 40-something charlie at her reunion &
my mom is hot enough to be stalked by every teen ex she had in the 80's
& not-so-popular charlie is a drab troll tr*mp supporter &
i guess hate doesn't age well idk but
maybe there is some justice in the world &
we can't see it when we're with people we don't really want to be with
in places we don't really want to be but
maybe when we grow up
we coalesce into the person we always were

to the really attractive tattooed t.s.a. man at the albuquerque, nm sunport

please do not open the box for my hot pink cardi b vibrator, this is an extremely open area, my mom is watching through the glass to ensure i make it to the other side, i am convinced you are probably the most beautiful man in all of albuquerque, you, a blue latex gloved early 2000s emo frontman, gerard way meets patrick swayze or *gerard wayze* as i've affectionately named you, everyone else in this airport looks like a southwestern adobe gutter troll, how are you even here? why are you handling my bag? maybe in a la la land twist of planetarium fate we both drift upward from the long steel table, some willy wonka fizzy lifting drink shit & the vibrator floats out of my bag & we dance to some caucasian orchestral symphony rodgers & hammerstein airport rave as we drift back to the ground you hold the vibrator in your hand & look lovingly into my soft gaze with a knowing stare that says you've been looking for a woman empowered by her own sexual freedom for some time now, my pink vibrator is the hottest thing about me, your heart is giving me a standing ovation & so! is! your! penis! i run back all the questions i had to ask at the sex shop, the amazon reviews i had to read, a single tear rolls gingerly down your face as you immortalize me as a hero in your memory, you tell me the most beatufiul thing about me is that i do not need you, that my freedom is self-sufficient & aware & bright fucking pink, that i know myself so well so that you might know me all the way, this sparkly ho heart is a dildo treasure chest, modicum of self love, a sculpture of survival i can hold in my hands, a man touched me once until i wished myself into all the untouched, this vibrator is a hum that says i am still here & i deserve consensual fucking orgasms & love & the way your bradley cooper hair falls in your face, maybe i deserve for you to open the box maybe it's time for the world to see me as the brave bad bitch i am, define myself as the thottie having more orgasms than u, i just went from hoping you wouldn't look at all to hoping you would whip that bitch out for the whole damn world to see, the right person wouldn't be intimidated by all my holy fem dildo jesus, the right person would pray to the soft pink saint of me, the right person would think i am the most radiant when i am free.

/fem renaissance/

get up, bitch/ you can't sleep 'til noon every day/ fuck daylight savings/ stop buying coffee at 4 PM/ you'll be drinking it until you can't sleep/ self care is not party dresses and chocolate chip cookies/ or is it?/ isn't it what you make it?/ bitch, I don't know !!/ today, you are instagram beat/ false lashes for no reason/ ariana grande's "thank u, next" meets carly rae jepsen's "party for one"/ fem renaissance/ cherry lip gloss/ hair straightener wave/ waterbed tummy/ hips, a full vase/ wide enough to greenhouse/ all of your blooming/ tattoo a tour of the country 'cross your shoulders/ leave a lipstick message on every mirror you find yourself in/ this life was never about anyone else/ you will only ever be a ghost of yourself/ today/ you are taki taki rumba/ cardi b verse/ *kinda scary/ hard to read/ like a ouija board/* linda ronstadt grito to the moon/ 8th grade dance/ all by yourself/ grabbing your own wallflower hand/ this is a love song/ for all the french fries you eat in the name of self care/ dresses bought in the name of body/ holy place/ maybe you have no party to wear them to/ maybe you are the fucking party/ you are every prom you were never invited to/ bouquets of flowers given to other girls/ fuck all that/ you are an orchard/ sweet apple blossom/ you are the space outside/ of arms that never held you/ like a sacred thing/ girl of your own dreams/ bruja mermaid/ reina de la luna/ ever surrounded/ by star stuff/ constellations for veins/ you are holding your own hand/ at the most romantic part of the movie/ telling yourself how beautiful you look/ in the rain/ you have written so many love letters/ for men who turned to salt/ alcohol/ a space you could no longer fit yourself into/ where is your manifesto?/ you love like the sandia mountains/ watermelon sky/ tender enough/ to turn a rigid thing soft/ pink/ blushing/ for the whole world to see/ why have you never given yourself the sky?

lessons i learned from selena

i sing "como la flor" at karaoke
and this is no longer a saloon in brooklyn
the crowd sings along with all of the spanish words
they don't really know, my t-shirt turns pearl-smattered bustier
and I become a grammy-award winning bellow
a-a-ayy como me duele...

lessons i learned from selena:

1. if you leave a chicken in the house, there will be caca everywhere
2. always eat an entire medium pizza by yourself
3. when the white boutique women won't sell you any clothes,
    make your own, start a busti-caca runway revolution,
    bedazzle until your brown is so loud, you can sew it into a dress
    tell them you won't be needing theirs after all

4. god bless the holiness that is purple
    disco jumpsuit ass, bless the brown girl butt
    bless all of its cumbia and washing machine hips
    praise all of its curves and peaks
    revolve around it
    they call it the moon for a reason

5. love is the red runaway car
    it is the holster of hot sauce and the twelve second kiss
    sometimes, it is a trashed hotel room and an angry father
    sometimes, it is a mother's acrylic nails running through your hair
    sometimes, you have to sing about all of its hurt

6. sometimes, brown is not brown enough
    when the world expects you to be double-tongued and ideal latina
    you make them love you anyway
    you spanglish your way into a smile
    you show them what a spanish song sounds like
    coming out of your mouth

7. after the death of selena, candles were lit all over the world
    while her music blasted through car windows
    howard stern played her songs under the sound of open fire
    calling them tasteless and weak, this is nothing new
    there will always be white men trying to silence us with their bullets
        there will always be bullets

8. all i can think is that we are the same age
    that all the brown girl stories i know
    end in accidents and early death
    my mother sings linda ronstadt from the next room
    my grandmother is frida kahlo, molded into hospital bed
    and we are surviving and we are alive
    like the bus wreck that did not kill gloria estefan
    like the rhythm that will not get us, the history that will not repeat
    como la flor, we will never die
    despite the lies that pay for guns over counters
    despite the world that only names us legends after we are gone
    we will sing love songs to ourselves so that our hearts never break
    until the whole world can't help
    but sing along with our every emotion
    even our deepest hurt

como la flor con tanto amor
me diste tu se marchito me marcho hoy yo se perder
pero a-a-ay, como me duele, a-a-ay, como me duele...

Great Aunt Carmen died today

& she was 98 & it was all very mexican, her sister, Esperanza, could
not forgive her for some unspeakable mentirosa puta hermana type
thing & Esperanza is about to be 100, stubborn as fuck, like fuck yes to
the mariachi birthday, the big band & a margarita with five straws &
a stripper because she's never had one & it isn't fair, yes, to the cumbia
she will dance like her hips have not ground into the bone of her, dance,
like the survival of the first abusive fucker was just a sorry tap routine
like the bueno green chile truck didn't slide the great love of her life
to his early death after he'd already beaten the war, after she thought
she'd won all of hers too, baila esta cumbia to erase the nightmares
of her lover's accident, her daughter, soon to follow, hydroplaned into
paralysis, wrists flicked like every spoon she lifted to my grandmother's
mouth, catholic tv church every sunday, telenovela at four, honey
bunches of oats hidden in the shower to keep them away from pinche
grandchildren, watch her wave like the flame of every candle lit for the
santos, how many times did she ask St. Anthony to help her find every
missing thing? did she ever get back all she lost? Great Aunt Carmen
died today & Esperanza is my middle name & i worry about the day
Esperanza will die too, my mother says it might be soon, that she only
wanted to outlive her sister, stubborn like the river feigning existence
in the desert & isn't that the most mexican thing? staying alive when it
feels like no one wants you to? defying everything that could kill you
just to prove a point?

on the first sunday of lent,

pastor judy says to come to the front if the spirit moves you, if you're looking for healing, so i move & my forehead is anointed with oil & i have bangs so my hair is just greasy now, i wonder if jesus' hair was greasy & maybe that's why he was so holy & shiny all the time, i make this joke whenever i go to church with my family about how none of it really applies to me because i'm a witch, it's not a joke, i went to the colorado river looking for yemaya when i moved, set up my altar with de la rosa mazapan & candles for selena, frida kahlo & barbara streisand, i am the femmetacostal congregation at my own xicana church, as i'm waiting in line to be healed i become acutely aware that i have forgotten how to pray, lost in the sunken sad of myself, my therapist says i am a dark room looking for a flashlight, my other therapist says to remember all the mermaid magazine cover of me, the holiest thing i can think of is the fact that i woke up this morning, scrolled the bible of instagram makeup tutorial and painted myself into parable, blessed be my chrome blue hoops, vintage denim with all the patches, choosing the bowie platforms over slip ons, blessed be my sideshave, noserings, weird tattoos, blessed be my breath choosing when to be poem & love song & joke, blessed be my brave breath choosing to steady when i am assaulted out of my own hometown, blessed be my brave breath when my lover turned to alcohol & anger, the holiest thing i can think of is the fact that i woke up this morning, blessed be my brave breath when i am forsaken but get back up anyway, love anyway, fight anyway, blessed be my brave breath when i do not want to breathe, unlovable sin, collapsed on the floor in ideation, the holiest thing i can think of is the fact that i am still alive, sparkling & spicy as ever, flexing on the past like a sorry bad boyfriend, blessed be my brave breath when i get behind the mic, when i am bullied but try again anyway, when i suture my scars into more than enough, blessed be my lipstick poems, my big stupid heart, my weird pinky toes, blessed be a prayer that says you did not break me, you will not break me, i am so fucking alive, blessed be a prayer that says i will wake up tomorrow, i got shit to do, i'm not done here, blessed be my small cat, blessed be my fear, blessed be my ache, blessed be the glow up that follows, the nights i nickname myself moon, the hundreds of people in the audience listening, the holiest thing i can think of is the fact that i am still alive & that is so so much more than enough *amen amen amen.*

when you go to olive garden alone/
they still give you a big fuckin salad/
basket of four breadsticks/ garlic salt/ a promise/
that i will ask for four more/
when i thought nobody liked me/
sat in a puddle of/ prom rejections/ useless/
axe body spray boys/ unworthy / i learned/
to go alone/ first safe place/ alfredo sanctuary/
give us our daily bread/
mountain of parmesan/
self reclamation/ peach bellini bad bitch/
i have my order memorized/ for the sad days/
full belly days/
the days i need to know/
i can make it/ all on my own

the parable of hospitaliano

ode to milk bar

i am watching chef's table
christina tosi
all birthday sprinkles & cornflakes
suddenly,
a boy appears
opening the grate
the east village store
he turns to face front
& i remember
waiting for that boy to come home
i remember the neon pink sign
blushing my cheeks
his not-so-indiscrete flirting
losing my favorite jeans in his apartment
i don't know how or why he
ended up on my television right now
but i do become acutely aware of the fact
that it has been a year
that i used to sit in the window
of the second ave milk bar
while he closed the store
my purse full
with blueberries and cream
double chocolate
the birthday cake truffles
from his freezer
in truth,
i didn't move here for him
i think i did it for the cookies
for cereal milk
for the first time i tasted something
i swore was churned by my own heart
i have made these desserts from scratch
i wanted everyone to know
what my feelings taste like
these bites will never
stop being synonymous with new york
my greatest love

the boy
was just a thoroughfare
dessert before the meal
i remember when my grandfather
gave me the family empanada recipe
how food is sometimes
the only way we know love
i sing along to waitress
messy kind
find myself in a recipe
the box for a brand new
tiffany blue kitchen aid mixer
i eat and remember
settled into
a cereal milkshake with extra crunch
thankful that I took the first bite
elated that it brought me here
opening up the grate
to all of this

taurus season is like craving a corn dog &
finding an extra corn dog in ur drive thru bag like the sun came back
from a bad breakup all glow & shine & stay so bright you forget every
bad thing taurus season is a thrift store haul to make a fake hipster
jealous where everything was a dollar taurus season is easter lace &
crisp crinoline the saccharine sweet howl of little gay church laughter
taurus season is that entire new lizzo album multiple friends sending
you articles about olive garden sending you poems saying you yes you
i see you i see all that broken as brave i am proud of you ok taurus
season is that good orgasm you've been waiting for sour patch kids
& peanut butter m&ms at the movies u couldn't decide so u got both
tiny wildflower bouquet from the cracked dry earth like woah look
how you bloomed when there was nothing around to water you pin it
in my hair call it a festival look celebration of survival taurus season is
like my birthday is the entire month of may !!! watch me tiara !! crown
myself amelia mignonette thermopolis renaldi princess! of! genovia!
on the hunt for a real foot poppin kiss michael moscovitz makeout
sesh shallow playing in the background & my lips poem his lips taurus
season is when he looks at me like bradley cooper looked at lady gaga
at the oscars like maybe the whole rest of the world is fucked but this
moment isn't like candle flickers while i read my song lyrics all slam
poet-like taurus season is my weird black hole hometown all squished
into the tiniest twinkling view like stars too close together dotting our
mouths while we storytell & shit talk taurus season is good secrets
slumber party giggled like we are here & i trust you i trust you the
dizzy slip into becoming the rosé cider i said i wouldn't drink for fear of
appearing basic taurus season is 80s prom pastel punk show too tight
jeans that suck yr butt into shape the graceful acceptance of another
year finally getting to bloom after all the empty sad seasons taurus
season is fuck i do not feel ready to be but i love to bloom i have to
plant just want to grow more & more of this

burn it all

after ada limón

say i can't pay rent
or electricity or water or phone bill
say i never stop getting fired
say i never find the exact right place at the exact right time
say they won't neuter my cat because i make a dollar too much
say i eat a lot of tuna
say i've been burned out for the last four years how
can i still be burning?
say they turn my high school home into a very important gas station
say when will they gentrify the mountains?
say i do not know how to do my taxes
say i am still sad tomorrow
say i cannot hold it down with iced coffee
say i eat gummy bears for dinner
say you leave, say i leave to see if it'll make me feel less alone
say all i do is leave or at least that's what it feels like
say i do not know how to person
say alone is not on my resume
say i always get fired from it too
collect unemployment
say i don't make it after all
say i am not all the things i thought i'd be
say somehow it will all be ok
say fuck it
say we roll around in the grass
say we stare down everything that will kill us
say we post it on instagram & make out
take a very sexy bath in all the bills we didn't pay
recreate that scene from *pretty woman*
say we run & run & run
say we stop
watch it all burning, the prettiest sunset
say we have a picnic watch the sky go down
watch it all
go down

gigi bella // is an award winning poet, theater artist and social justice advocate. She has been ranked the tenth woman poet in the world (WOWPS 2017). She is the two time Project X Bronx Poetry Champion as well as a literal mermaid. She is a Pink Door Fellow, a National Poetry Champion and Semifinalist, and is ranked within the top 25 teams in the nation at the 2018 National Poetry Slam and was part of the first ever all Latinx Project X Bronx Slam Team. She has been featured on stages with Andrea Gibson, Clementine Von Radics, Sabrina Benaim, Lauren Zuniga, Olivia Gatwood and many others. Her chapbook, *weird things*, was featured on the instagram of pop singer/songwriter, Sara Bareilles ("Love Song," "Brave," Waitress the Musical). Her other work is featured in What Are Birds? and is forthcoming in Maps for Teeth and Knight's Library.